Pebble® Plus

Hands-On Science Fun

How to Build a

FIZZY ROCKET

Revised Edition

by Lori Shores

Consultant: Ronald Browne, PhD
Department of Elementary & Early Childhood Education
Minnesota State University, Mankato

CAPSTONE PRESS
a capstone imprint

4D
Download the Capstone 4D app for additional content.

4D See page 2 for directions.

Download the Capstone 4D app!

- Ask an adult to search in the Apple App Store or Google Play for "Capstone 4D".
- Click Install (Android) or Get, then Install (Apple).
- Open the app.
- Scan any of the following spreads with this icon:

When you scan a spread, you'll find fun extra stuff to go with this book!
You can also find these things on the web at www.capstone4D.com
using the password: **rocket.09434**

Pebble Plus is published by Capstone Press,
1710 Roe Crest Drive, North Mankato, Minnesota 56003
www.mycapstone.com

Library of Congress Cataloging-in-Publication Data
is available on the Library of Congress website.

ISBN 978-1-5435-0943-4 (library binding)
ISBN 978-1-5435-0949-6 (paperback)
ISBN 978-1-5435-0955-7 (ebook pdf)

Editorial Credits
Marissa Kirkman, editor; Sarah Bennett, designer;
Tracy Cummins, media researcher; Tori Abraham,
production specialist

Photo Credits
Capstone Studio: Karon Dubke, Cover, 1, 3, 5, 7, 9, 11, 13, 15, 17,
19, 21; Otto Rogge Photography: 4–5 (sky); Shutterstock:
art-sonik, Design Element Cover and Interior, BkPoop Photo,
1 (sky)

Note to Parents and Teachers

The Hands-On Science Fun set supports national science
standards related to physical science. This book describes and
illustrates building a fizzy rocket. The images support early
readers in understanding the text. The repetition of words and
phrases helps early readers learn new words. This book also
introduces early readers to subject-specific vocabulary words,
which are defined in the Glossary section. Early readers may
need assistance to read some words and to use the Table of
Contents, Glossary, Read More, Internet Sites, Critical Thinking
Questions, and Index sections of the book.

Printed and bound in the United States of America.
010772S18

Table of Contents

Safety Note:
Please ask an adult for help in building and launching your fizzy rocket.

Getting Started

Rockets blast off into space. You can use simple materials to launch your own rocket into the air.

Here's what you need:

tape

safety glasses

8.5" x 11" (22 cm x 28 cm) sheet of paper

scissors

white plastic film canister with a lid that fits inside (available anywhere film is developed or online)

½ of a fizzing antacid tablet made with sodium bicarbonate

1 teaspoon (5 mL) warm water

Making a Fizzy Rocket

Cut the paper in half.

One half will be the body
of the rocket.

Tape the edge of the paper to the upside down film canister.

Form the paper into a tube.

Tape down the other edge of paper.

Cut a circle from the other half
of paper. Cut a slit, and overlap
the sides to form a cone.
Tape the cone on top of the tube.

Cut out two triangles, and
tape them to the tube for fins.

Put on safety glasses,
and turn over the rocket.

Then add 1 teaspoon (5 mL)
of warm water to the canister.

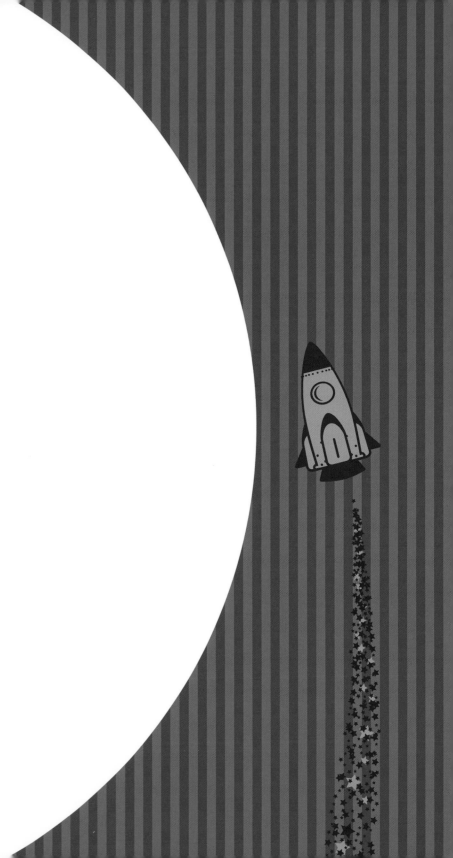

13

Take the rocket, lid,

and antacid outside.

Drop the half tablet

of antacid into the water.

Snap the lid on right away.

Quickly stand up the rocket.

Step back about 6 feet
(2 meters) to watch.

How high will the rocket go?

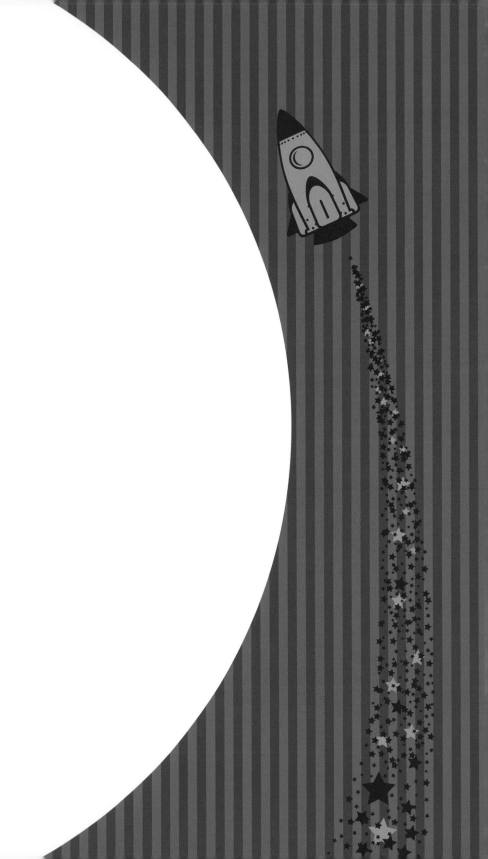

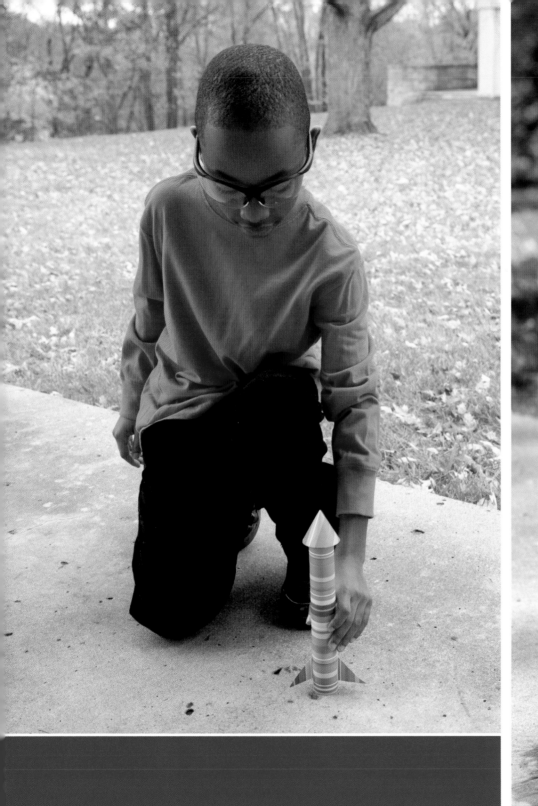

How Does It Work?

A reaction started when the antacid tablet and water mixed. The water and the tablet made little bubbles of gas.

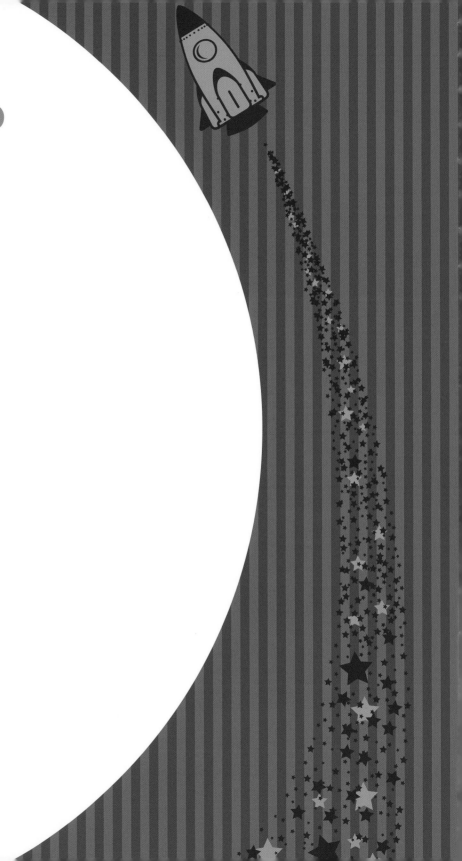

gas bubbles

Soon the canister filled with gas. Pressure inside the canister made the lid pop off. As gas rushed out, the canister was pushed into the air.

Glossary

antacid—a medicine that reduces the amount of acid in your stomach to soothe an upset stomach

fin—a small, triangular structure on a rocket used to help with steering

gas—a substance, such as air, that spreads to fill any space that holds it

launch—to send a rocket into space

material—the thing from which something is made

pressure—a force made by pressing on something

reaction—an action in response to something that happens

Read More

Heinecke, Liz Lee. *Outdoor Science Lab for Kids: 52 Family-Friendly Experiments for the Yard, Garden, Playground, and Park.* Beverly, Mass.: Quarry Books, 2016.

Oyler, Amy. *Pop, Sizzle, Boom!: 101 Science Experiments for the Mad Scientist in Every Kid.* New York: St. Martin's Press, 2017.

Smibert, Angie. *Mind-Blowing Physical Science Activities.* Curious Scientists. North Mankato, Minn.: Capstone Press, 2018.

Internet Sites

Use FactHound to find Internet sites related to this book.

Visit *www.facthound.com*

Just type **9781543509434** and go.

Super-cool stuff!

Check out projects, games and lots more at
www.capstonekids.com

Critical Thinking Questions

1. What two items caused a reaction when they were mixed together?

2. What caused the lid to pop off of the canister?

3. What pushed the rocket into the air?

Index